Table
TALK

Table
TALK

QUESTIONS and QUOTES to START
HUNDREDS of GREAT FAMILY DISCUSSIONS
on PATRIOTISM, VALUES, FUN, and FAITH

JOHN and TINA BUSHMAN

PLAIN SIGHT PUBLISHING
AN IMPRINT OF CEDAR FORT, INC.
SPRINGVILLE, UTAH

© 2013 John and Tina Bushman

ISBN 13: 978-1-4621-1146-6

Published by Plain Sight Publishing, an imprint of Cedar Fort, Inc.
2373 W. 700 S., Springville, UT 84663
Distributed by Cedar Fort, Inc., www.cedarfort.com

LIBRARY OF CONGRESS CATALOGING-IN-PUBLICATION DATA

Bushman, John S. (John Stanford), 1971- author.
Table talk : questions and quotes to start hundreds of great family discussions on patriotism, values, fun, and faith / John and Tina Bushman.
    pages cm
Includes bibliographical references and index.
Summary: Questions and quotes to start hundreds of family discussions on patriotism, values, fun, and faith.
ISBN 978-1-4621-1146-6 (alk. paper)
1. Table-talk. 2. Conversation. 3. Communication in families. I. Bushman, Tina, author. II. Title.

HQ734.B933 2013
302.34'6--dc23

                                    2012044974

Cover design by Erica Dixon
Cover design © 2013 by Lyle Mortimer
Edited and typeset by Whitney A. Lindsley

Printed in the United States of America

10 9 8 7 6 5 4 3 2 1

INTRODUCTION

HOW do you change the world for good? That is a difficult question, but there is no question of where to start.

A man decided that he would change the world.

But, he wasn't successful.

So he decided to change the country.

But, he wasn't successful.

So he decided to change his community.

But, he wasn't successful.

So he decided to change his street.

But, be wasn't successful.

So he decided to change his family.

INTRODUCTION

But, he wasn't successful.

So he decided to change himself.

And he was successful.

And his family changed and they affected their street.

And the people on the street affected their community.

And the people of the community affected their country.

And the people of the country affected the world.

—*Author unknown (used by Glenn Beck)*

THIS book focuses on that change within us and our families. Like Ronald Reagan said, "All great change in America begins at the dinner table."

Nothing has a greater or more lasting impact on children than their parents, yet our society tries to weaken that influence. Activities, friends, work, school, TV, and social media are all competing for our children's attention and trying to replace us as their teachers. Social commentator Zbigniew Brzezinski observed:

"Television . . . has replaced the family, the school, and the church—in that order—as the principal [instrument] for socialization and transmission of values. . . . Greed, debauchery, violence, unlimited self-gratification, absence of moral restraint . . . are the daily fare glamorously dished up to our children." ("Weak Ramparts of the Permissive West," in Nathan P. Gardels, ed., *At Century's End: Great Minds*

Reflect on Our Times [1995)], 53).

Table Talk is filled with fun and insightful questions that will help families accomplish two important goals: to assist in establishing healthy lines of communication and to help your family identify, crystallize, and transmit family values and expectations.

The first goal is to assist in establishing healthy lines of communication. This is especially crucial during the challenges our children will certainly face. As children develop a pattern of talking with their parents, they will be able to turn to their parents in times of need. You will be amazed at how the questions and quotes contained in this book will bring out meaningful discussions. In a lighthearted yet interesting manner, this book presents questions that will help your family get to know each other and explore ideas.

Researchers have found a strong connection between family communication and later behavior of family members. Dr. Blake Bowden from Cincinnati Children's Hospital used a survey of 527 teenagers to see how their families and lifestyles affected their individual mental health and adjustment. The study found "that adolescents whose parents ate dinner with them five times per week or more were the least likely to be on drugs, depressed, or in trouble with the law. They were also more likely to be doing well in school and surrounded by a supportive circle of friends. The more poorly adjusted teens had parents who ate with them only three evenings per week or less" (see Dobson, *Bringing Up Boys*, 92). Certainly, dinnertime is not the only time to communicate in a family, but it can be a effective and enjoyable time together.

The second goal is to help your family identify, crystallize, and transmit family values and expectations. Children are "dished up" and "served" many positive and negative values each day from so many different sources. In today's society, we as parents must be careful to ensure those values are consistent with our family's beliefs and goals. Making an effort to better communicate will ensure that our family values and norms are the most prevalent and

---

powerful in our children's lives.

The questions and quotations in this book will help your family learn about and explore

- Patriotism, politics, and good government (I know that last one seems to be an oxymoron)

- Faith, beliefs, and morals

- Education and the value of hard work

- Preparedness and safety

- Family, friends, and relationships

- Each other's interests, ideas, and personalities and other questions to help you get to each other better. (Just have fun together!)

So whether at the dinner table, in the car, at bedtime, or any other time, pull out *Table Talk* to learn together about values and each other.

QUICK TIPS FOR GREAT TABLE TALKS

TIP #1: Questions teach better than answers. As parents, we often have a tendency to try to answer every question when a discussion comes up. We may even break into lecture mode. In reality, children usually know what the right answers are and just need a chance to express them. Rather than lecturing, we should draw the answers out of our children. One great educator, Emma Goldman, said, "Education is a process of drawing out, not of driving in."

For instance, if a parent says, "Smoking is awful because . . ." a child might want to tune out the lecture. On the other hand, if a parent asks, "What do you think are some bad effects that come from smoking?" a child will be more likely to pay attention because the answers are

---

coming from himself. As a child processes a question, he begins to internalize his beliefs and values. By verbally expressing his beliefs, he will discover that he really believes them. Consequently, his decisions and beliefs will become a part of him. He will also remember what is said much longer because he was the one saying it. It's surprising to see how well kids come up with the right answers.

TIP #2: The questions are not meant to control discussion but rather to spark and promote discussion. Don't limit yourselves to the questions on the page. Follow up with a "how?" or "why?" Allow the questions to act as a springboard to discuss anything.

TIP #3: Build confidence. Don't grill your children, just the burgers. Make it so that family members will feel free to express themselves without being ridiculed or criticized. Children will be afraid to answer if they feel that an answer will be made fun of or will start a fight. Try to steer away from arguments

QUICK TIPS FOR GREAT TABLE TALKS

---

and keep it a neutral discussion. If someone's understanding is wrong, it is more likely that his or her belief will change naturally over time, rather than with someone aggressively opposing that opinion.

If you could choose to be famous, what would you want to be famous for?

a. Sports
b. Art
c. Music
d. Science
e. Politics
f. Other

"Always do your best. What you plant now, you will harvest later."

—*Og Mandino, speaker and author*

"People who are unable to motivate themselves must be content with mediocrity, no matter how impressive their other talents."

—*Andrew Carnegie, entrepreneur*

Have you ever had someone close to you die, such as a friend or family member?

- What were your feelings at that time?

- What do you believe happens to a person's soul when they die?

"It is the will of God and Nature that these mortal bodies be laid aside, when the soul is to enter into real life; 'tis rather an embryo state, a preparation for living; a man is not completely born until he be dead: Why then should we grieve that a new child is born among the immortals?"

—*Benjamin Franklin, founding father and inventor*

"My most embarrassing moment was when _____."

"Accept that all of us can be hurt, that all of us can and surely will at times fail. Other vulnerabilities, like being embarrassed or risking love, can be terrifying, too. I think we should follow a simple rule: if we can take the worst, take the risk."

—*Joyce Brothers, advice columnist*

Besides voting, what are ways to be politically active?

- Why is it important to be politically active?
- What are other areas of society we should be actively involved in?

"All that is necessary for the triumph of evil is that good men do nothing."

—*Edmund Burke, Irish statesman*

"Evil is powerless if the good are unafraid."

—*Ronald Reagan, fortieth US president*

What calamity or natural disaster is most likely to occur where you live?

- Are you prepared?
- Does every family member know what to do in case of such an incident?

"Hope for the best, but prepare for the worst."

—Old English proverb

What roles do virtue and moral values play in the strength of a nation?

"A general dissolution of principles and manners will more surely overthrow the liberties of America than the whole force of the common enemy. While the people are virtuous they cannot be subdued; but when once they lose their virtue then will be ready to surrender their liberties to the first external or internal invader."

—*Samuel Adams, founding father*

What is the strangest or most exotic
food you have ever tried?

- What exotic or strange food do you
  think would be fun to try?
- What food do you think you could
  never eat?

"Red meat is not bad for you. Now, blue-green
meat, that's bad for you!"

—*Tommy Smothers, American comedian
and composer*

"Everything I eat has been proved by some doctor
or other to be a deadly poison, and everything I
don't eat has been proved to be indispensable for
life. But I go marching on."

—*George Bernard Shaw, Irish playwright*

How does a person know if
he or she is in love?

- How is romantic love different than
  friendship love or family love?

"If you love somebody, let them go. If they return,
they were always yours. If they don't, they never
were."

—*David Harkins, English poet*

"Other things may change us, but we start and
end with family."

—*Anthony Brandt, writer*

What are the best ways to make changes in the government and its leaders?

- Why would violence be the absolute last resort to avoid tyranny?

- Why is peaceful protest so effective?

"Please be peaceful. We believe in law and order. We are not advocating violence, I want you to love your enemies . . . for what we are doing is right, what we are doing is just—and God is with us."

—*Martin Luther King, Jr., civil rights leader and preacher*

"Above all, we must realize that no arsenal, or no weapon in the arsenals of the world, is so formidable as the will and moral courage of free men and women. It is a weapon our adversaries in today's world do not have."

—*Ronald Reagan, fortieth US president*

What are some good charitable organizations to give to?

- How should we decide what is the right amount to give?

"I do not believe one can settle how much we ought to give. I am afraid the only safe rule is to give more than we can spare. . . . If our charities do not at all pinch or hamper us, I should say they are too small. There ought to be things we should like to do and cannot do because our charitable expenditures excludes them."

—*C. S. Lewis, English author and scholar*

"Verily I say unto you, Inasmuch as ye have done it unto one of the least of these my brethren, ye have done it unto me."

—*Jesus Christ, Matthew 25:40 KJV*

If you could have a personal servant do any of the following things, which would you choose?

a. Clean the house
b. Chauffeur the whole family
c. Cook
d. Be your secretary
e. Other

"I'm a great believer in luck, and I find the harder I work the more I have of it."

—*Thomas Jefferson, founding father and third US president*

What would you do to make the world a better place?

- How can you prepare to make a difference in the world?

"To every man there comes . . . that special moment when he is figuratively tapped on the shoulder and offered the chance to do a special thing unique to him and fitted to his talent. What a tragedy if that moment finds him unprepared or unqualified for the work which would be his finest hour."

—*Winston Churchill, British prime minister during World War II*

13

What should you do if you see that the house is on fire?

- Where would your family meet to make sure everyone is out of the house safely?

"Don't let your dreams go up in smoke—practice fire safety."

—Author unknown

"If you play with fire, you're gonna get burned."

—Author unknown

"How is it that one match can start a forest fire, but it takes a whole box of matches to start a campfire?"

—Christy Whitehead

Why is thrift a virtue?

- Why should you save money and not spend every dime you earn?

"I believe that thrift is essential to well-ordered living."

—*John D. Rockefeller, entrepreneur and philanthropist*

"Beware of little expenses. A small leak will sink a great ship."

—*Benjamin Franklin, founding father and inventor*

"Credit buying is much like being drunk. The buzz happens immediately and gives you a lift. . . . The hangover comes the day after."

—*Joyce Brothers, advice columnist*

If you could remove the need for any of the following bodily needs, which would it be?

a. Sleeping
b. Eating
c. Bathing
d. Exercise
e. Other bathroom needs

"But godliness with contentment is great gain. For we brought nothing into this world, and it is certain we can carry nothing out. And having food and raiment let us be therewith content."

—*Apostle Paul, 1 Timothy 6:6–8 KJV*

"A true friend is someone who

_____."

"A friend is one who knows us, but loves us anyway."

—*Jerome Cummings, author and Catholic priest*

Should the rich pay a higher percent of their income in taxes?

- If so, what is the proper percent for the most wealthy?

- What are some dangers of taxing the rich too much?

"You cannot legislate the poor into freedom by legislating the industrious out of it. You don't multiply wealth by dividing it. Government cannot give anything to anybody that it doesn't first take from somebody else. Whenever somebody receives something without working for it, somebody else has to work for it without receiving. The worst thing that can happen to a nation is for half of the people to get the idea they don't have to work because somebody else will work for them, and the other half to get the idea that it does no good to work because they don't get to enjoy the fruit of their labor."

—*Dr. Adrian Rogers, pastor*

What part does prayer play in your life?

- When do you find yourself praying the most?
- How could your family improve with prayer?

"Confess your faults one to another, and pray one for another, that ye may be healed. The effectual fervent prayer of a righteous man availeth much."

—*James 5:16 KJV*

"Prayer is not overcoming God's reluctance, but laying hold of His willingness."

—*Martin Luther, leader of the Reformation*

"Don't pray when you feel like it. Have an appointment with the Lord and keep it. A man is powerful on his knees."

—*Corrie ten Boom, author and Holocaust survivor*

What is the furthest east you have ever traveled?

- West? North? South?
- What are some of your future travel plans?

"I have found out that there ain't no surer way to find out whether you like people or hate them than to travel with them."

—*Mark Twain, American author and humorist*

"Travel is fatal to prejudice, bigotry, and narrow-mindedness, and many of our people need it sorely on these accounts. Broad, wholesome, charitable views of men and things cannot be acquired by vegetating in one little corner of the earth all one's lifetime."

—*Mark Twain*

If you could go back to change
one event or decision of the
past, would you?

- What decision?
- Has that event or decision made you
  a better person?

"When one door closes, another opens; but we
often look so long and so regretfully upon the
closed door that we do not see the one which has
opened for us."

—*Alexander Graham Bell, inventor*

"Many of us crucify ourselves between two
thieves—regret for the past and fear of the future."

—*Fulton Oursler, American journalist
and writer*

~~How~~ difficult would it be to say no if you were offered drugs?

- What is a good way to say no if you are offered drugs?

"Let us not forget who we are. Drug abuse is a repudiation of everything America is."

—*Ronald Reagan, fortieth US President*

Have you ever stuck up for someone who was being picked on? Why?

• Are there times you should defend people you don't particularly like? When?

"In Germany, the Nazis first came for the communists, and I didn't speak up because I wasn't a communist. Then they came for the Jews, and I didn't speak up because I wasn't a Jew. Then they came for the trade unionists, and I didn't speak up because I wasn't a trade unionist. Then they came for the Catholics, but I didn't speak up because I was a Protestant. Then they came for me, and by that time there was no one left to speak for me."

—*Rev. Martin Niemoeller, German anti-Nazi theologian*

Who is your favorite author?

- What is the best book you have ever read?
- Why did you like it so much?

"A good book has no ending."

—*R. D. Cumming, author*

"The man who does not read good books has no advantage over the man who can't read them."

—*Mark Twain, American author and humorist*

Have you ever thought someone was good-looking the first time you met him or her, but the more you got to know that person, the less attractive he or she became?

- Have you ever experienced the opposite?

"That which is striking and beautiful is not always good, but that which is good is always beautiful."

—*Ninon de L'Enclos, French author*

"Beauty is . . . when you look into a woman's eyes and see what is in her heart."

—*Nate Dircks*

"Taking joy in living is a woman's best cosmetic."

—*Rosalind Russell, American actress*

What role should guns play in a society?

- Why do some want to limit the rights of others to bear arms?

- What limits should there be in bearing arms?

"A well regulated Militia, being necessary to the security of a free State, the right of the people to keep and bear Arms, shall not be infringed."

—*Second Amendment, US Constitution*

"Oppressors can tyrannize only when they achieve a standing army, an enslaved press, and a disarmed populace."

—*James Madison, founding father and fourth US president*

How has your belief in God changed over the course of your life?

- What does it mean to have God as the center of your life?

"And thou shalt love the Lord thy God with all thine heart, and with all thy soul, and with all thy might. And these words, which I command thee this day, shall be in thine heart: And thou shalt teach them diligently unto thy children, and shalt talk of them when thou sittest in thine house, and when thou walkest by the way, and when thou liest down, and when thou risest up."

—*Deuteronomy 6:5–7 KJV*

Do you think life exists on other planets?

- Do you believe the stories about alien contact?

"Babies have big heads and big eyes, and tiny little bodies with tiny little arms and legs. So did the aliens at Roswell! I rest my case."

—*William Shatner, Canadian actor*

"Our constitution protects aliens, drunks and U.S. Senators."

—*Will Rogers, American comedian and actor*

What is a goal you have?

- What are you doing to accomplish it?

"A winner is someone who recognizes his God-given talents, works his tail off to develop them into skills, and uses these skills to accomplish his goals."

—*Larry Bird, NBA basketball player and coach*

"Good habits formed at youth make all the difference."

—*Aristotle, Greek philosopher*

What should you do if someone is choking?

- What should you do if someone has stopped breathing?
- Have a family member research this.

If your house caught on fire and you could only save one non-living item, what would it be? Why?

"I conceive that the great part of the miseries of mankind are brought upon them by false estimates they have made of the value of things."

—*Benjamin Franklin, founding father and inventor*

At a state fair, what
would you enjoy most?

a. Roller coasters and rides
b. Carnival games
c. The food
d. The entertainment
e. The displays

• When was the last time you went to
  a state fair?

Parents: Tell about your first date together.

- How long was your engagement?
- What is your best memory from that time period?
- How did he propose?

"Love one another and you will be happy. It's as simple and as difficult as that."

—*Michael Leunig, Australian poet, cartoonist, and cultural commentator*

"We're all a little weird. And life is a little weird. And when we find someone whose weirdness is compatible with ours, we join up with them and fall into mutually satisfying weirdness—and call it love—true love."

—*Robert Fulghum, American author*

"Success in marriage does not come merely through finding the right mate, but through being the right mate."

—*Barnett R. Brickner, rabbi*

What role should the state or federal government play in helping the poor or those in need?

- How can well-intended programs for the needy cause more harm than good?

- What does your family do to help those in need?

"I am for doing good to the poor but I differ in opinion of the means. I think the best way of doing good to the poor, is not making them easy in poverty, but leading or driving them out of it. In my youth I travelled much, and I observed in different countries, that the more public provisions were made for the poor, the less they provided for themselves, and of course became poorer. And, on the contrary, the less was done for them, the more they did for themselves, and became richer."

—*Benjamin Franklin, founding father and inventor*

"Compassion is defined not by how many people are on the government dole but by how many people no longer need government assistance."

—*Rush Limbaugh, political commentator*

When is a time you have felt
God's Spirit most?

- What are things that often help you
  feel close to God?

"But the Comforter, which is the Holy Ghost,
whom the Father will send in my name, he shall
teach you all things, and bring all things to your
remembrance, whatsoever I have said unto you.
Peace I leave with you, my peace I give unto you:
not as the world giveth, give I unto you. Let not
your heart be troubled, neither let it be afraid."

—*Jesus Christ, John 14:26–27 KJV*

"For where two or three are gathered together in
my name, there am I in the midst of them."

—*Jesus Christ, Matthew 18:20 KJV*

"My favorite sport to watch is
_____."

"Sports is human life in microcosm."

—*Howard Cosell, American sports commentator*

"I wanted to have a career in sports when I was young, but I had to give it up. I'm only six feet tall, so I couldn't play basketball. I'm only 190 pounds, so I couldn't play football. And I have 20-20 vision, so I couldn't be a referee."

—*Jay Leno, comedian*

If you could choose any person in the world as your family's dinner guest, who would it be and why?

- What about anyone who has ever lived as your dinner guest?

"A single conversation with a wise man is better than ten years of study."

—*Chinese proverb*

"A hero is someone we can admire without apology."

—*Kitty Kelley, American journalist and biographer*

"A hero is someone who has given his or her life to something bigger than oneself."

—*Joseph Campbell, American writer*

What should you do in case of an earthquake?

- Type the question into your web browser and look for answers.

"We learn geology the morning after the earthquake."

—*Ralph Waldo Emerson, American author*

What is the biggest change you have made in your life for good?

"No matter how far you have gone on a wrong road, turn back."

—*Turkish proverb*

What is your worst experience with a bug?

"Nothing seems to please a fly so much as to be taken for a currant; and if it can be baked in a cake and palmed off on the unwary, it dies happy."

—*Mark Twain, American author and humorist*

Why do people like to gossip? What's the danger of gossiping?

"Whoever gossips to you will gossip about you."

—*Spanish proverb*

"The easiest way to keep a secret is without help."

—*Author unknown*

"There is so much good in the worst of us,
And so much bad in the best of us,
That it hardly behooves any of us
To talk about the rest of us."

—*Edward Wallis Hoch, former governor of Kansas*

Why did the founding fathers desire strong limits on the federal government?

• What dangers come from a large government?

"You can't be for big government, big taxes, and big bureaucracy and still be for the little guy."

—*Ronald Reagan, fortieth US president*

If you could travel into the future to visit for a few days, would you?

- How far into the future would you like to travel?

"Man . . . can go up against gravitation in a balloon, and why should he not hope that ultimately he may be able to stop or accelerate his drift along the Time-Dimension, or even turn about and travel the other way."

—*H. G. Wells, author of* The Time Machine

"If I had to trade places in life with someone, it would be with _____."

- Would you also want to take all of the circumstances of that person?

"The grass is not, in fact, always greener on the other side of the fence. Fences have nothing to do with it. The grass is greenest where it is watered. When crossing over fences, carry water with you and tend the grass wherever you may be."

—*Robert Fulghum, author*

How do cigarettes hurt you physically? Socially? Monetarily?

- What would be a good way to turn down someone who offered you a cigarette?

"One thousand Americans stop smoking every day—by dying."

—*Author unknown*

Which poor hygiene characteristic is the most offensive to you?

a. Unbrushed teeth
b. Body odor
c. Greasy hair
d. Dirty clothes
e. Other

"All places where women are excluded tend downward to barbarism; but the moment she is introduced, there come in with her courtesy, cleanliness, sobriety, and order."

—*Harriet Beecher Stowe, American abolitionist and author*

"When I got out of high school they retired my jersey, but it was for hygiene and sanitary reasons."

—*George Carlin, comedian*

If you had to eat the same thing every day, for every meal, for a year, what would you choose to eat?

"Part of the secret of success in life is to eat what you like and let the food fight it out inside."

—*Mark Twain, American author and humorist*

"Preheat the oven? Really? If I was the sort of person who planned ahead, I wouldn't be eating this Totino's Party Pizza in the first place."

—*Adam Peterson*

What are some traditions your family has during Easter, Passover, or other religious holidays?

"Family traditions counter alienation and confusion. They help us define who we are; they provide something steady, reliable and safe in a confusing world."

—*Susan Lieberman, psychologist*

Is it ever okay for a school or government agency to give advantages to some people based on their skin color or ethnic group?

- What are your feelings about affirmative action programs?

- How should those with disadvantages be helped?

"I have a dream that my four little children will one day live in a nation where they will not be judged by the color of their skin but by the content of their character."

—*Martin Luther King Jr., civil rights leader and preacher*

49

What is your favorite scripture verse?

- How could your family improve with scripture reading?

"The word of God hidden in the heart is a stubborn voice to suppress."

—*Billy Graham, American evangelist*

"It is impossible to rightly govern the world without God and the Bible."

—*George Washington, first US president*

"This book of the law shall not depart out of thy mouth; but thou shalt meditate therein day and night, that thou mayest observe to do according to all that is written therein: for then thou shalt make thy way prosperous, and then thou shalt have good success."

—*Joshua 1:8 KJV*

50

What kind of book do you most enjoy?

a. Fantasy
b. History
c. Humor
d. Nonfiction
e. Mystery
f. Romance
g. Science Fiction
h. Other

• When is the last time you read one of those kinds of books?

"The worth of a book is to be measured by what you can carry away from it."

—*James Bryce, British academic, historian, and politician*

"Anyone who says they have only one life to live must not know how to read a book."

—*Author unknown*

If you could have any job or profession in the world, what would it be? Why?

- What part does money play in your choice?
- Would you change your mind if all professions paid the same?

"When people go to work, they shouldn't have to leave their hearts at home."

—*Betty Bender, former president of the Library Administration and Management Association*

Which of the following items do you have in case of emergency?

a. Extra food
b. Clean water
c. Warm clothing
d. First aid kit
e. Fire extinguisher
f. Cash

"It wasn't raining when Noah built the ark."

—*Howard Ruff, financial adviser and writer*

Imagine your family is only going to have five TV channels (network or cable) but together you can choose which five your family will have.

- See if you can come to a consensus as a family on which five channels your family will share.

- What are the virtues and vices of television?

"A genuine leader is not a searcher for consensus but a molder of consensus."

—*Martin Luther King Jr., civil rights leader and preacher*

"All television is educational television. The question is: what is it teaching?"

—*Nicholas Johnson, former FCC commissioner*

What is the worst vacation experience you have ever had?

- What was the best vacation experience you have ever had?

"No man needs a vacation so much as the person who has just had one."

—*Elbert Hubbard, American writer and philosopher*

"A good vacation is over when you begin to yearn for your work."

—*Morris Fishbein, physician and editor*

How do you know if you
can trust someone?

- How long does it take before you
  generally trust someone?

"You may be deceived if you trust too much, but
you will live in torment unless you trust enough."

—*Frank Crane, American actor and director*

What is the purpose of government?

- What purposes did the founding fathers list in the preamble of the Constitution?

"We the People of the United States, in order to form a more perfect Union, establish Justice, insure domestic Tranquility, provide for the common defense, promote the general Welfare, and secure the Blessings of Liberty to ourselves and our Posterity, do ordain and establish this Constitution for the United States of America."

—*Preamble of the United States Constitution*

- Do people now feel government should try to do more? How?

Parents: When you were growing up, what role did going to church play in your family, if any?

• Does church play a more or less active role in your family now? Why?

"And let us consider how we may spur one another on toward love and good deeds, not giving up meeting together, as some are in the habit of doing, but encouraging one another—and all the more as you see the Day approaching."

—*Hebrews 10:24–25 NIV*

When shopping for clothes,
what do you look at first?

a. Style
b. Price
c. Name brand
d. Size

"The finest clothing made is a person's skin, but, of course, society demands something more than this."

—*Mark Twain, American author and humorist*

"If men liked shopping, they'd call it research."

—*Cynthia Nelms, American artist*

What is an achievement you would like to accomplish in life?

• What keeps people from achieving great things?

"Fear is the thief of dreams."

—Author unknown

60

What would you do if a friend of yours seems depressed and has mentioned that he has considered suicide?

"Suicide is a permanent solution to a temporary problem."

—*Phil Donahue, talk show host*

If a friend came to you wearing a ridiculous outfit and asked how he or she looked, what would you do?

a. Tell him or her you like it to avoid hurting any feelings
b. Be totally honest
c. Politely tell them you don't like it
d. Cleverly change the subject
e. Other

"Those who think it is permissible to tell white lies soon grow color-blind."

—*Austin O'Malley, American physicist*

"When you stretch the truth, watch out for the snapback."

—*Bill Copeland, American poet, writer, and historian*

What kind of boat would
you like to have?

a. Sailboat
b. Ski boat
c. Canoe or kayak
d. Fishing boat
e. Other

"Sticks and stones may break my bones, but words can never hurt me."

- Have you found this saying to be true?

- Have a person's words ever hurt you more deeply than breaking a bone would?

How does someone legally immigrate to our country?

- How does someone illegally immigrate?
- What dangers can come from illegal immigration?

"Illegal immigration is a crisis for our country. It is an open door for drugs, criminals, and potential terrorists to enter our country. It is straining our economy, adding costs to our judicial, healthcare, and education systems."

—*Timothy Murphy, US congressman*

"We all learned in kindergarten that the beginning is a very good place to start. As we have this debate on illegal immigration and illegal entry into this country, let's begin at the very beginning by sealing the borders to this great Nation."

—*Marsha Blackburn, US congresswoman*

If you had to lose one of your five senses, which would you choose?

a. Smell
b. Sight
c. Hearing
d. Touch
e. Taste

- If you could only keep one sense, which would it be?

"Common Sense is that which judges the things given to it by other senses."

—*Leonardo da Vinci, great mind of the Renaissance*

What kinds of things do you find fun to learn about?

"You can teach a student a lesson for a day; but if you can teach him to learn by creating curiosity, he will continue the learning process as long as he lives."

—*Clay P. Bedford, American businessman*

What should you do if you have become a victim of sexual abuse?

- Whom should you tell?

"Abuse changes your life . . . Fight Back and change the life of your abusers by Breaking Your Silence on Abuse!"

—*Patty Rase Hopson, cofounder LavenderPower.org*

What is the opposite of blaming?

• Why is taking personal responsibility so important?

"Nobody ever did, or ever will, escape the consequences of his choices."

—*Alfred A. Montapert, author*

"You must take personal responsibility. You cannot change the circumstances, the seasons, or the wind, but you can change yourself. That is something you have charge of."

—*Jim Rohn, American entrepreneur*

Have you ever experienced dèjá vu? When?

"I went into a fancy French restaurant called 'Déjà vu.' The head waiter said, 'Don't I know you?'"

—*Rod Schmidt*

Fill in the blank about the person to the left of you.

"I love your _____."

"Appreciation is a wonderful thing: It makes what is excellent in others belong to us as well."

—*Voltaire, French philosopher*

Do you feel there is ever justification for someone to have an abortion?

- Under what circumstances do you feel that an abortion is acceptable?

- What part, if any, do you feel government should play with abortion? Should they help fund them?

"Simple morality dictates that unless and until someone can prove the unborn human is not alive, we must give it the benefit of the doubt and assume it is [alive]. And, thus, it should be entitled to life, liberty, and the pursuit of happiness."

—*Ronald Reagan, fortieth US president*

Do you believe in miracles?

- Have you ever seen or experienced a miracle? When?

"Miracles are not contrary to nature, but only contrary to what we know about nature."

—*Saint Augustine, philosopher and theologian*

Would you rather the weather be very hot or very cold?

- Would your response likely change six months from now?

"The trouble with weather forecasting is that it's right too often for us to ignore it and wrong too often for us to rely on it."

—*Patrick Young, Scottish scholar*

"To be interested in the changing seasons is a happier state of mind than to be hopelessly in love with spring."

—*George Santayana, Spanish-American philosopher*

What chores are you responsible for in your house?

- Which do you least enjoy?
- Which do you not mind as much?

Parents: Share about the chores you had growing up.

"Housework is something you do that nobody notices until you don't do it."

—*Author unknown*

"Nature abhors a vacuum. And so do I."

—*Anne Gibbons, cartoonist*

What advice would you give to someone being picked on at school?

- What would you do if some kids were picking on someone else at school?

"Bullies are always cowards at heart and may be credited with a pretty safe instinct in scenting their prey."

—*Anna Julia Cooper, African-American author and scholar*

"Injustice anywhere is a threat to justice everywhere."

—*Martin Luther King, Jr., civil rights leader and preacher*

What is the hardest work
you have ever done?

- What satisfaction has come to you
  through working hard?

"Opportunity is missed by most people because it
is dressed in overalls and looks like work."

—*Thomas Edison, American inventor*

When was the last time you cried?

* When was the last time you cried laughing?

"Laughter and tears are both responses to frustration and exhaustion. I myself prefer to laugh, since there is less cleaning up to do afterward."

—*Kurt Vonnegut, American writer*

"To weep is to make less the depth of grief."

—*William Shakespeare, English playwright,*
in King Henry VI

What do you think is the most important element of a strong marriage?

- What things can a person do to keep a marriage strong?

"What counts in making a happy marriage is not so much how compatible you are, but how you deal with incompatibility."

—*Leo Nikolaevich Tolstoy, Russian writer*

What responsibilities do individual states have?

- What responsibilities does the federal government have?

"I consider the foundation of the [Federal] Constitution as laid on this ground: That 'all powers not delegated to the United States, by the Constitution, nor prohibited by it to the States, are reserved to the States or to the people.' [10th Amendment] To take a single step beyond the boundaries thus specifically drawn around the powers of Congress is to take possession of a boundless field of power, no longer susceptible of any definition."

—*Thomas Jefferson, third US president and founding father*

"The powers delegated by the proposed Constitution to the federal government are few and defined. Those which are to remain in the State governments are numerous and indefinite."

—*James Madison, fourth US president and founding father*

What is your favorite scripture story?

• Why do you like it?

"And that from a child thou hast known the holy scriptures, which are able to make thee wise unto salvation through faith which is in Christ Jesus."

—*Apostle Paul, 2 Timothy 3:15 KJV*

What do you think is the easiest time of life?

a. Childhood
b. Adolescence
c. College age
d. Middle age
e. Senior citizen

"You are as young as your faith, as old as your doubt; as young as your self-confidence, as old as your fear; as young as your hope, as old as your despair."

—*Douglas MacArthur, US Army general*

"How old would you be if you didn't know how old you were?"

—*Satchel Paige, American baseball player*

Parents: What was your first paying job?

- How did you get this job?
- Describe your responsibilities, salary, and boss.

"Find a job you like and you add five days to every week."

—*H. Jackson Brown Jr., American author*

What are your thoughts about gun safety?

- What are the best ways to teach gun safety?

- Search for "gun safety" in your web browser and share some tips you find.

Parents: How have you seen moral standards in society change in your lifetime?

- What dangers are there in the idea that we can change the moral standards?

"No one man, however brilliant or well-informed, can come in one lifetime to such fullness of understanding as to safely judge and dismiss the customs or institutions of his society, for those are the wisdom of generations after centuries of experiment in the laboratory of history."

—*Will and Ariel Durant, American authors*

What is a joke you have heard recently?

- What is your all-time favorite joke?

"Imagination was given to man to compensate him for what he is not; a sense of humor to console him for what he is."

—*Francis Bacon, English statesman*

"If I had no sense of humor, I would long ago have committed suicide."

—*Mahatma Gandhi, leader of the India Independence Movement*

"He who laughs, lasts."

—*Mary Pettibone Poole, author*

What indoor games did you enjoy when you were growing up?

- What is your favorite indoor game now?

- When is the last time you played one of those games?

"Cards are war, in disguise of a sport."

—*Charles Lamb, English essayist*

"The perfect family board game is one that can be played each time with fewer pieces."

—*Robert Brault, American writer*

Why might private citizens and private companies spend money more efficiently than governments do?

"Millions of individuals making their own decisions in the marketplace will always allocate resources better than any centralized government planning process."

—*Ronald Reagan, fortieth US president*

What do you think is the purpose of families?

- What part do families play in our faith in God?

"A family is a place where principles are hammered and honed on the anvil of everyday living."
—*Charles R. Swindoll, American evangelist*

"A happy family is but an earlier heaven."
—*George Bernard Shaw, Irish playwright*

If you could magically wake up tomorrow and be an expert at any sport, what would it be and why?

· Do you usually like team or individual sports?

"The more I practice, the luckier I get."
—*Jerry Player, American professional golfer*

"The key is not the 'will to win'—everybody has that. It is the will to prepare to win that is important."
—*Bobby Knight, American basketball coach*

Have you ever been inspired to be a better person because of the example of someone else? Who?

- Has the example of another person ever discouraged you?
- What kind of example do you think you are to others?

"Example moves the world more than doctrine. The great exemplars are the poets of action, and it makes little difference whether they be forces for good or forces for evil."

—Henry Miller, *American novelist and painter*

What damage comes from sharing sexual intimacy before marriage?

- What are some guidelines about sexual relations?
- What dangers are there from early sexual relations, physically, socially, psychologically, and economically?

"A youth boiling with hormones will wonder why he should not give full freedom to his sexual desires; and if he's unchecked by custom, morals or laws, he may ruin his life before he matures sufficiently to understand that sex is a river of fire that must be banked and cooled by a hundred restraints if it is not to consume in chaos both the individual and the group."

—*Will and Ariel Durant, authors*

Have you ever wondered if
you were adopted?

- Were you adopted?
- Would you ever adopt and under what circumstances?

"Biology is the least of what makes someone a mother."

—*Oprah Winfrey, American show host*

"Not flesh of my flesh, Nor bone of my bone,
But still miraculously my own.
Never forget for a single minute,
You didn't grow under my heart—but in it."

—*Fleur Conkling Heylinger, poet*

What is the worst accident or injury you have ever had?

• What helped you in your recovery?

"And lest I should be exalted above measure through the abundance of the revelations, there was given to me a thorn in the flesh, the messenger of Satan to buffet me, lest I should be exalted above measure. For this thing I besought the Lord thrice, that it might depart from me. And he said unto me, My grace is sufficient for thee: for my strength is made perfect in weakness."

—*Apostle Paul, 2 Corinthians 12:7–9 KJV*

How does the government
get itself into debt?

- How is this similar to how a family
  gets into debt?

- How do families and governments
  get out of debt?

"We don't have a trillion-dollar debt because we
haven't taxed enough; we have a trillion-dollar
debt because we spend too much."

—*Ronald Reagan, fortieth US president*

If God or an angel appeared to you, do you think it would make you want to be a better person? Why or why not?

"Faith is a passionate intuition."

—*William Wordsworth, English poet*

"Faith . . . must be enforced by reason. . . . When faith becomes blind, it dies."

—*Mahatma Gandhi, leader of the India Independence Movement*

"Now faith is the substance of things hoped for, the evidence of things not seen."

—*Hebrews 11:1 KJV*

What is your favorite part of the day?

a. Getting up
b. Going to bed
c. Eating lunch
d. Going to work
e. Coming home
f. Working out
g. Other

- What is your least favorite part of the day?

"This is the day which the Lord hath made; we will rejoice and be glad in it."

—*Psalms 118:24 KJV*

If you could wake up tomorrow knowing another language, what language would you choose?

- What other language is most useful in your community?
- Is sign language useful in your community?

"If you talk to a man in a language he understands, that goes to his head. If you talk to him in his own language, that goes to his heart."

—*Nelson Mandela, politician and former president of South Africa*

"You can never understand one language until you understand at least two."

—*Geoffrey Willians, author*

Kids: What should you do if an adult in a car politely asks you to help him find a lost pet?

• Run away and tell an adult.

"Take heed that ye despise not one of these little ones; for I say unto you, That in heaven their angels do always behold the face of my Father which is in heaven."

—*Jesus Christ, Matthew 18:10 KJV*

When do you find it most difficult to be honest?

a. At school
b. At work
c. With family
d. With friends

If you left a store and realized that a cashier gave you too much change, what would you do?

- What if the cashier didn't give you enough change?

"No man has a good enough memory to make a successful liar."

—*Abraham Lincoln, sixteenth US president*

If you could eat at any restaurant in the world tonight, where would it be?

"The age of your children is a key factor in how quickly you are served in a restaurant. We once had a waiter in Canada who said, 'Could I get you your check?' and we answered, 'How about the menu first?'"

—*Erma Bombeck, newspaper columnist*

Do you believe in love at first sight?

- What about the first time you held one of your children?

"Beauty is not in the face; beauty is a light in the heart."

—*Kahlil Gibran, Lebanese-American artist*

Why is limited government important?

- Why might governments and organizations try to draw power to themselves?

"I hope we have once again reminded people that man is not free unless government is limited. There's a clear cause and effect here that is as neat and predictable as a law of physics: as government expands, liberty contracts."

—*Ronald Reagan, fortieth US president*

- Why does expanded government decrease liberties and freedoms?

"I believe there are more instances of the abridgement of the freedom of the people by gradual and silent encroachments of those in power than by violent and sudden usurpations."

—*James Madison, fourth US president and founding father*

What do you think heaven is like?

- What do you think hell is like?
- In descriptions of heaven and hell, what things do you think are metaphorical? What things are literal?

"And God shall wipe away all tears from their eyes; and there shall be no more death, neither sorrow, nor crying, neither shall there be any more pain: for the former things are passed away. . . . Behold, I make all things new. And he said unto me, Write: for these words are true and faithful. . . . He that overcometh shall inherit all things; and I will be his God, and he shall be my son. But the fearful, and unbelieving, and the abominable, and murderers, and whoremongers, and sorcerers, and idolaters, and all liars, shall have their part in the lake which burneth with fire and brimstone: which is the second death."

—*Apostle John, Revelation 21:4–8 KJV*

If you had to wear the same color of clothing for the rest of your life, which color would you choose?

"If men can run the world, why can't they stop wearing neckties? How intelligent is it to start the day by tying a little noose around your neck?"

—*Linda Ellerbee, American journalist*

105

If you had all the money you wanted and needed, would you continue to work?

- What would you do with your time?
- What have you learned from hard work?

"Many people quit looking for work when they find a job."

—*Author unknown*

What would you do if you found out your closest friend was using drugs?

"Kids who learn a lot about the risks of drugs from their parents are 50% less likely to use drugs."

—*The Partnership at Drugfree.org*

What was your favorite TV show when you were younger?

- How has media changed since then?
- What are standards in your family for what you can watch or how long you can watch?

"If you came and you found a strange man . . . teaching your kids to punch each other, or trying to sell them all kinds of products, you'd kick him right out of the house, but here you are; you come in and the TV is on, and you don't think twice about it."

—*Jerome Singer, American psychologist*

What is your favorite type of cookie?

"Cookies are made of butter and love."

—*Norwegian proverb*

Where were you born?

- Do you know where your parents were born? Grandparents? Siblings?

"In every conceivable manner, the family is a link to our past, bridge to our future."

—*Alex Haley, American author*

What role does our country have with foreign policy besides protecting its own borders and protecting its economic interests?

- What role does our country have in the global community?

"Here is my first principle of foreign policy: good government at home."

—*William E. Gladstone, British statesman and prime minister*

"How did we win the election in the year 2000? We talked about a humble foreign policy: No nation-building; don't police the world. That's conservative, it's Republican, it's pro-American—it follows the founding fathers. And, besides, it follows the Constitution."

—*Ron Paul, US congressman*

- When did those ideas change with the George W. Bush administration? For better or worse?

What part did God have with the founding of our nation?

- How did the founding fathers feel about God?

- What role should God play in our nation today?

- What role does he play?

"God governs in the Affairs of Men. And if a sparrow cannot fall to the ground without his notice, is it probable that an Empire can rise without His Aid? We have been assured . . . in the Sacred Writings, that except the Lord build the House they labor in vain who build it. I firmly believe this, – I also believe that, without His concurring Aid, we shall succeed in this political Building no better than the builders of Babel."

—*Benjamin Franklin, founding father and inventor*

"Blessed is the nation whose God is the Lord."

—*Psalm 33:12 KJV*

What is the best April Fools'
trick you have ever played or
had played on you?

- What is the best April Fools' trick
  you have ever heard of?

"April 1. This is the day upon which we are
reminded of what we are on the other three hundred and sixty-four."

—*Mark Twain, American author and humorist*

"The trouble with practical jokes is that very often
they get elected."

—*Will Rogers, American actor and comedian*

What are some good ways to overcome feeling sad?

"Anger is just a cowardly extension of sadness. It's a lot easier to be angry at someone than it is to tell them you're hurt."

—*Tom Gates*

"The walls we build around us to keep sadness out also keeps out the joy."

—*Jim Rohn, American speaker and author*

"You cannot prevent the birds of sadness from passing over your head, but you can prevent their making a nest in your hair."

—*Chinese proverb*

Have you ever experienced any of the following calamities or natural disasters?

a. Earthquake
b. Flood
c. Major house fire
d. Hurricane
e. Tornado
f. Typhoon

- Were you prepared for it? Tell about it.
- Which of these does your family need to prepare better for?

"Be prepared."

—*Boy Scout motto*

If you were given a million dollars to give away in your name, what two organizations would you contribute to?

"Philanthropy is commendable, but it must not cause the philanthropist to overlook the circumstances of economic injustice which make philanthropy necessary."

—*Martin Luther King Jr., civil rights leader and preacher*

"Billions are wasted on ineffective philanthropy. Philanthropy is decades behind business in applying rigorous thinking to the use of money."

—*Michael Porter, Harvard Business School professor*

What is your favorite dessert?

"'Stressed' spelled backwards is 'desserts.' Coincidence? I think not!"

—*Author unknown*

"Life is uncertain. Eat dessert first."

—*Ernestine Ulmer*

"Without ice cream, there would be darkness and chaos."

—*Don Kardong, American runner and author*

"Man cannot live on chocolate alone, but woman sure can."

—*Author unknown*

What is your idea of an ideal date?

- What is the most creative date you have ever been part of?
- What do you think is the right age to start dating?

"Watching your daughter being collected by her date feels like handing over a million-dollar Stradivarius to a gorilla."

—*Jim Bishop, American writer*

What is capitalism?

- Why does capitalism work? Why doesn't socialism?

"America's abundance was created not by public sacrifices to the common good, but by the productive genius of free men who pursued their own personal interests and the making of their own private fortunes. They did not starve the people to pay for America's industrialization. They gave the people better jobs, higher wages, and cheaper goods with every new machine they invented, with every scientific discovery or technological advance—and thus the whole country was moving forward and profiting, not suffering, every step of the way."

—*Ayn Rand, Russian-American novelist*

"The inherent vice of capitalism is the unequal sharing of blessings; the inherent virtue of socialism is the equal sharing of miseries."

—*Winston Churchill, British prime minister during World War II*

Which is the "Golden Rule"?

a. Do unto others as they have done unto you.

b. Do unto others according to what they deserve.

c. Do unto others as you would have others do unto you.

d. Do unto others before they can do it unto you.

e. Avoid others because they might do something unto you.

"Therefore all things whatsoever ye would that men should do to you, do ye even so to them: for this is the law and the prophets."

—*Jesus Christ, Matthew 7:12 KJV*

What kind of shopping do you like the most?

a. Grocery
b. Clothes
c. Electronics
d. Music and video
e. Home improvement
f. Other

"Shopping: The fine art of acquiring things you don't need with money you don't have."

—*Author unknown*

"My all-time favorite teacher was
_____."

- Why did you like that teacher so much?

"The dream begins with a teacher who believes in you, who tugs and pushes and leads you to the next plateau, sometimes poking you with a sharp stick called 'truth.'"

—*Dan Rather, American journalist*

"A teacher is one who makes himself progressively unnecessary."

—*Thomas Carruthers*

"When you teach your son, you teach your son's son."

—*The Talmud*

122

Have you ever had to
put out a grease fire?

- What is the proper way to put out a grease fire?

- Unless you have a lot of baking soda ready, or a chemical fire extinguisher, try covering the fire with a lid. Water will tend to spread the fire. Research more tips on the Internet.

Dear Problem Solver,

Some friends and I stole some candy from the store. We ate it, and it wasn't even that good. Now I feel pretty bad about it. What should I do?

"A thief believes everybody steals."

—*Edgar Watson Howe, American novelist*

If you could have any superpower,
what would it be?

"With great power comes great responsibility."

—*Peter Parker's Uncle Ben*
(from Spider-Man)

Who was your best friend during elementary school?

- Who was your best friend in junior high and in high school? Do you still talk with him or her?

"The friend is the man who knows all about you, and still likes you."

—*Elbert Hubbard, American writer*

"A friend is one of the nicest things you can have, and one of the best things you can be."

—*Douglas Pagels*

"The antidote for fifty enemies is one friend."

—*Aristotle, Greek philosopher*

What liberties and freedoms do we sometimes give up for greater safety and security?

• Airports are an example.

"Those who would give up Essential Liberty to purchase a little Temporary Safety, deserve neither Liberty nor Safety."

—Benjamin Franklin, founding father and inventor

• Is there a difference between "Essential Liberty" and conveniences?

Why does God allow bad things to happen to good people?

"And we know that all things work together for good to them that love God."

—Apostle Paul, Romans 8:28 KJV

"For he [God] maketh his sun to rise on the evil and on the good, and sendeth rain on the just and on the unjust."

—Jesus Christ, Matthew 5:45 KJV

What do you think has been the most significant invention that has happened in your lifetime?

- What do you think is the most significant invention ever?
- What is one modern invention that you feel you could not live without?

"To invent, you need a good imagination and a pile of junk."

—*Thomas Edison, American inventor*

"The best way to predict the future is to invent it."

—*Alan Kay, American computer scientist*

What type of museum would you enjoy most?

a. History museum
b. Science museum
c. Art museum
d. Dinosaur museum
e. Archeology museum

• When is the last time you visited a museum?

"Give me a museum and I'll fill it."

—*Pablo Picasso, Spanish artist*

Kids: What would you do if someone touched you somewhere they shouldn't (where a bathing suit would go)?

• Whom should you tell?

"The consequences of your denial will be with you for a lifetime and will be passed down to the next generations. Break your Silence on Abuse!"

—*Patty Rase Hopson, cofounder, LavenderPower.org*

What are your feelings about swearing?

- Are there some swear words that are worse than others?

- Are there circumstances when using a swear word is okay?

- Do you feel differently about girls swearing?

"The foolish and wicked practice of profane cursing and swearing is a vice so mean and low that every person of sense and character detests and despises it."

—*George Washington, first US president*

Which of the following modern conveniences are you most grateful for?

a. Water heater
b. Indoor plumbing
c. Dishwasher
d. Washer
e. Dryer
f. Heater
g. Air conditioner
h. Telephone

"There is no such thing as gratitude unexpressed. If it is unexpressed, it is plain, old-fashioned ingratitude."

—*Robert Brault, American writer*

Who is one of your favorite relatives?

"Nobody has ever before asked the nuclear family to live all by itself in a box the way we do. With no relatives, no support, we've put it in an impossible situation."

—*Margaret Mead, American cultural anthropologist*

"Families are like fudge—mostly sweet with a few nuts."

—*Author unknown*

When do government laws and regulations become a problem?

- What things should the government regulate?

"That government is best which governs the least, because its people discipline themselves."

—*Thomas Jefferson, founding father and third US president*

"The nine most terrifying words in the English language are, 'I'm from the government and I'm here to help.'"

—*Ronald Reagan, fortieth US president*

"Government is not the solution to our problem. Government *is* the problem."

—*Ronald Reagan, fortieth US president*

What do you think the world will be like in fifty years?

- Will it be a better place or worse?

- Do you believe that Christ will have come within the next fifty years?

- If he doesn't come, would that affect the answer to the second question?

"But of that day and hour knoweth no man, no, not the angels of heaven, but my Father only. But as the days of Noe were, so shall also the coming of the Son of man be. For as in the days that were before the flood they were eating and drinking, marrying and giving in marriage, until the day that Noe entered into the ark, and knew not until the flood came, and took them all away; so shall also the coming of the Son of man be."

—*Jesus Christ, Matthew 24:36–39 KJV*

If you could witness any event
in world history, what event
would you choose?

"If you want to understand today, you have to search yesterday."

—*Pearl S. Buck, American author*

"History with its flickering lamp stumbles along the trail of the past, trying to reconstruct its scenes, to revive its echoes, and kindle with pale gleams the passion of former days."

—*Winston Churchill, British prime minister during World War II*

What is a talent you have?

- What talent or ability would you like to suddenly have?

- If you had to work hard to achieve that talent or ability, would you change your answer?

"Obstacles are those frightful things you see when you take your eyes off your goal."

—*Henry Ford, American inventor*

"One half of knowing what you want is knowing what you must give up before you get it."

—*Sidney Howard, American playwright*

Why is wearing a seatbelt in a car a good idea?

- Has a seatbelt ever helped someone you know in an accident?

"Safety doesn't happen by accident."

—*Author unknown*

"Safety is a cheap and effective insurance policy."

—*Author unknown*

"Hug your kids at home, but belt them in the car."

—*Author unknown*

How do you feel about hunting?

- Do you feel hunting is okay in order to control a population of animals so they don't overgraze or starve?

"People never lie so much as after a hunt, during a war or before an election."

—*Otto von Bismarck, German statesman*

Have you ever played
a musical instrument?

- What musical instrument would
  you like to learn how to play?

"Take a music bath once or twice a week for a few seasons. You will find it is to the soul what a water bath is to the body."

—*Oliver Wendell Holmes, American author*

What countries did your ancestors come from?

- Who was the first ancestor you know of to come to this country and from where?

"A people without the knowledge of their past history, origin and culture is like a tree without roots."

—*Marcus Garvey, American journalist*

What kinds of things should
a nation go to war over?

"War is an ugly thing, but not the ugliest of things. The decayed and degraded state of moral and patriotic feeling which thinks that nothing is worth war is much worse. The person who has nothing for which he is willing to fight, nothing which is more important than his own personal safety, is a miserable creature and has no chance of being free unless made and kept so by the exertions of better men than himself."

—*John Stuart Mill, British philosopher*

Have you ever made a deal with God to get you out of a bad situation?

- Did it work?
- Did you keep your end of the deal?

"We're given second chances every day of our life. We don't usually take them, but they're there for the taking."

—*Andrew M. Greeley, Irish-American Catholic priest*

What is the biggest surprise you have ever had?

"The secret to humor is surprise."

—*Aristotle, Greek philosopher*

"Surprise is the greatest gift which life can grant us."

—*Boris Pasternak, Russian poet*

Parents: What clubs, organizations, activities, or sports did you participate in during high school?

- Do you wish you did more or less?

"I pay the schoolmaster, but 'tis the schoolboys that educate my son."

—*Ralph Waldo Emerson, American poet*

Parents: Did your family have any home remedies for common sicknesses (earaches, headaches, hiccups, colds, and so on)?

• Does your family still use those remedies?

"There is a remedy for everything except death."
—*Miguel de Cervantes Saavedra, Spanish writer*

What is the best gift you have ever been given?

- What is the best gift you have ever given?

- What does the following quote by Ralph Waldo Emerson mean to you?

"Rings and other jewels are not gifts, but apologies for gifts. The only gift is a portion of thyself."

—*Ralph Waldo Emerson, American poet*

What is your favorite season? Why?

a. Summer
b. Winter
c. Spring
d. Fall

"It was one of those March days when the sun shines hot and the wind blows cold: when it is summer in the light, and winter in the shade."

—*Charles Dickens, English novelist*

Parents: How old were you when you got married?

- How old were your parents when they got married?
- What is a good age to get married?

"Chains do not hold a marriage together. It is threads, hundreds of tiny threads which sew people together through the years."

—*Simone Signoret, French actress*

Why should a nation have a strong military even when it is not at war?

"History teaches that war begins when governments believe the price of aggression is cheap."

—*Ronald Reagan, fortieth US president*

"Speak softly and carry a big stick, and you will go far."

—*Teddy Roosevelt, twenty-sixth US president*

If you were forced to leave the country with your family and never return, what other country would you choose to live in? Why?

"I like to see a man proud of the place in which he lives. I like to see a man live so that his place will be proud of him."

—*Abraham Lincoln, sixteenth US president*

'My God! How little do my countrymen know what precious blessings they are in possession of, and which no other people on earth enjoy!"

—*Thomas Jefferson, founding father and third US president*

152

What are the dangers of pornography to an individual?

- What are the dangers of pornography to a family and society?

"Movies are attempting to destroy something that's supposed to be the most beautiful thing a man and a woman can have by making it cheap and common."

—*Nancy Reagan, American First Lady*

"Internet pornography is often the first exposure that children and teens have to sexual images. This plants in them a twisted and perverse view of human intimacy that is difficult or impossible to weed out. These early learning experiences can lead to sexual deviancy and crime, and often negatively affect their future relationships and marriages."

—*Mark Kastleman*

What type of vacationing would you enjoy most?

a. Beach
b. Mountains
c. Big city
d. Cruise
e. Boating
f. Theme park
g. Other

"In America there are two classes of travel—first class, and with children."

—*Robert Benchley, American humorist*

If God came to you in a dream and told you to leave all and go live on a remote island alone, would you do it?

- Do you have limits on what God could ask of you?

- What if he told you to sacrifice your son like he told Abraham to do in Genesis 22?

"But what things were gain to me, those I counted loss for Christ. Yea doubtless, and I count all things but loss for the excellency of the knowledge of Christ Jesus my Lord: for whom I have suffered the loss of all things, and do count them but dung, that I may win Christ, and be found in him, not having mine own righteousness, which is of the law, but that which is through the faith of Christ, the righteousness which is of God by faith: That I may know him, and the power of his resurrection, and the fellowship of his sufferings, being made conformable unto his death."

—*Apostle Paul, Philippians 3:7–10 KJV*

Which US president do you think has done the most for our country?

- Which has hurt our country the most?

"Power tends to corrupt, and absolute power corrupts absolutely."

—*Lord Acton, British historian*

When have you most wanted to get revenge?

- What is wrong with trying to get revenge?

"He that studieth revenge keepeth his own wounds green, which otherwise would heal and do well."

—*John Milton, English poet*

"An eye for an eye and a tooth for a tooth and the world will be blind and toothless."

—*Mahatma Gandhi, leader of the India Independence Movement*

When should you call 911?

- You should call 911 when you have an emergency. An emergency is considered an immediate threat to persons and/or property.

What is your favorite hobby or pastime?

- What pastime or hobby would you like to take up?

"A man practices the art of adventure when he breaks the chain of routine and renews his life through reading new books, traveling to new places, making new friends, taking up new hobbies and adopting new viewpoints."

—*Wilfred Peterson*

If you knew the world would end in two weeks, what would you do?

- Would your answer change if the ending of the world was Christ coming to destroy the wicked and save the righteous in two weeks?

"He which testifieth these things saith, Surely I come quickly. Amen. Even so, come, Lord Jesus."

—*Apostle John, Revelation 22:20, KJV*

How do you feel when people
burn your country's flag as
a way to protest?

- Do you feel people have a right to
  express themselves in this way as
  part of their freedom of speech?

"We do not consecrate the flag by punishing its
desecration, for in doing so we dilute the freedom
that this cherished emblem represents."

—*William J. Brennan, US Supreme Court Justice*

If you knew you were going to die very soon, what would you want to say or write to your family?

• What is stopping you from saying those things now?

"At the end of your life, you will never regret not having passed one more test, not winning one more verdict or not closing one more deal. You will regret time not spent with a husband, a friend, a child, or a parent."

—*Barbara Bush, US First Lady*

How does one develop
greater willpower?

- What are some situations where will
  power or delayed gratification are
  very important characteristics?

"Don't give up what you want most for what you
want now."

—*Author unknown*

If you could travel back in time
and change one world event,
what would it be?

"People are trapped in history, and history is
trapped in them."

—*James Baldwin, American writer*

What do you believe about angels?

- What powers do you think they have?
- Do you believe in guardian angels?
- Do you think you have ever met one and not known it?

"Be not forgetful to entertain strangers: for thereby some have entertained angels unawares."

—*Hebrews 13:2 KJV*

If you needed to join the military, but were given the choice of which branch to join, which of the following would you choose?

a. Army
b. Navy
c. Air Force
d. Marines
e. Coast Guard

"People sleep peaceably in their beds at night only because rough men stand ready to do violence on their behalf."

—*George Orwell, English author*

What is your favorite type of music?

- What types of music did you listen to when you were younger?

"Without music life would be a mistake."

—*Friedrich Wilhelm Nietzsche,*
German philosopher

"A painter paints pictures on canvas. But musicians paint their pictures on silence."

—*Leopold Stokowski, British orchestral conductor*

What is your favorite holiday?

- How do you like to celebrate it?
- Did you feel differently when you were younger?

"It's like your children talking about holidays, you find they have a quite different memory of it from you. Perhaps everything is not how it is, but how it's remembered."

—*Denis Norden, English humorist*

"A perpetual holiday is a good working definition of hell."

—*George Bernard Shaw, Irish playwright*

What type of art do you like best?

• What kind of art don't you appreciate?

"It has been said that art is a tryst, for in the joy of it maker and beholder meet."

—*Kojiro Tomita*

If you could ask God one question, what would your question be?

"Any fool can count the seeds in an apple. Only God can count all the apples in one seed."

—*Robert H. Schuller, American evangelist*

"Every evening I turn my worries over to God. He's going to be up all night anyway."

—*Mary C. Crowley*

"God loves each of us as if there were only one of us."

—*Saint Augustine, philosopher and theologian*

What is our responsibility toward protecting the environments of animals and plant life?

- What stewardship has God given to man in regards to the environment?

"And God said, Let us make man in our image, after our likeness: and let them have dominion over the fish of the sea, and over the fowl of the air, and over the cattle, and over all the earth, and over every creeping thing that creepeth upon the earth."

—*Genesis 1:26 KJV*

"I care not much for a man's religion whose dog and cat are not the better for it."

—*Abraham Lincoln, sixteenth US president*

When was a defining moment in your life, a moment that changed who you were and what you would become?

"When we are no longer able to change a situation, we are challenged to change ourselves."

—*Viktor Frankl, Austrian psychiatrist and Holocaust survivor*

What do you think is the most important factor to consider in a career choice?

a. Money
b. Love for the job
c. Hours
d. Location

"Nobody can go back and start a new beginning, but anyone can start today and make a new ending."

—*Maria Robinson*

"Life can either be accepted or changed. If it is not accepted, it must be changed. If it cannot be changed, then it must be accepted."

—*Author unknown*

What is your favorite type of food?

a. Mexican
b. Italian
c. French
d. German
e. Chinese
f. Japanese
g. American
h. Other

"When I'm at a Chinese restaurant having a hard time with chopsticks, I always hope that there's a Chinese kid at an American restaurant somewhere who's struggling mightily with a fork."

—*Rick Budinich*

If a genie appeared to you and offered to grant you one wish, what would you wish for? (No wishing for more wishes.)

- Would you ask the same thing if it were God appearing to you?

"Keep praying, but be thankful that God's answers are wiser than your prayers!"

—*William Culbertson, American entrepreneur*

What political party do you lean toward?

- What are some of the views this party represents?

- Would you ever vote for someone of another party?

- Who did you vote for in the last election? Why?

"If a political party does not have its foundation in the determination to advance a cause that is right and that is moral, then it is not a political party; it is merely a conspiracy to seize power."

—*Dwight D. Eisenhower, thirty-fourth US president*

What might be some difficulties that could come from being very wealthy?

- Would you like to take the risks anyway?

"For we brought nothing into this world, and it is certain we can carry nothing out. And having food and raiment let us be therewith content. But they that will be rich fall into temptation and a snare, and into many foolish and hurtful lusts, which drown men in destruction and perdition. For the love of money is the root of all evil: which while some coveted after, they have erred from the faith, and pierced themselves through with many sorrows."

—*Apostle Paul, 1 Timothy 6:7–10 KJV*

Dear Problem Solver,

I would like to make some close friends but I am not sure where to start. What should I do to make some good friends?

"The only way to have a friend is to be one."

—*Ralph Waldo Emerson, American author*

"Show me your friends, and I'll show you your future."

—*Author unknown*

If you could magically live in any time in history, when would you choose?

- Where would you want to live?

"America is another name for opportunity. Our whole history appears like a last effort of divine providence on behalf of the human race."

—*Ralph Waldo Emerson, American author*

Have you ever had an enemy that
later became a friend?

• What is the nicest thing you have
ever done for an enemy?

"But I say unto you, Love your enemies, bless
them that curse you, do good to them that hate
you, and pray for them which despitefully use
you, and persecute you."

—*Jesus Christ, Matthew 5:44 KJV*

How do you feel about
the death penalty?

- Are there some forms of the death penalty that you feel are more humane than others?

Are there lawsuits that you believe are
frivolous and should be thrown out?

• Would you participate in one of
them if there were a large amount of
money to be made?

Which of the following do you wish you had more time for?

a. Work
b. Family
c. Sleeping
d. TV
e. Friends
f. Hobbies

- Looking back at the end of your life, do you think you would make the same choices of how to spend your time?

"In reality, killing time is only the name for another of the multifarious ways by which Time kills us."

—*Osbert Sitwell, English writer*

What is the last dream you can remember?

- What is the most memorable dream you have ever had?

- Do you think there is any significance to dreams?

- How do you feel about dream interpretation?

"Dreams are only thoughts you didn't have time to think about during the day."

—*Author unknown*

"Dreaming permits each and every one of us to be quietly and safely insane every night of our lives."

—*William Dement, sleep researcher*

Who do you think is the most influential religious leader since biblical times? Why?

- Who do you think is the most influential religious leader of other world religions besides Christianity?

Which civil right do you feel most grateful for?

a. Freedom of speech and press
b. Freedom to worship according to your own convictions
c. Freedom to bear arms
d. Other

"The Framers of the Bill of Rights did not purport to 'create' rights. Rather, they designed the Bill of Rights to prohibit our Government from infringing rights and liberties presumed to be preexisting."

—*William J. Brennan, US Supreme Court Justice*

What are your feelings about tattoos or body piercings?

- What are consequences that can come from tattoos and body piercings?

"The world is divided into two kinds of people: those who have tattoos, and those who are afraid of people with tattoos."

—*Author unknown*

"Your body is a temple, but how long can you live in the same house before you redecorate?"

—*Author unknown*

How would you most enjoy celebrating your birthday?

- Tell about a birthday party that you remember.

"There is still no cure for the common birthday."

—*John Glenn, American astronaut and senator*

"We know we're getting old when the only thing we want for our birthday is not to be reminded of it."

—*Author unknown*

If you were to be reincarnated as an animal, which would you choose?

- What kind of animals would best represent the other members of your family?

"I used to believe in reincarnation, but that was long ago, in another life."

—*Dave Schinbeckler*

Of all of the commandments, which do you feel is the most important? Why?

"Then one of them, which was a lawyer, asked him a question, tempting him, and saying, Master, which is the great commandment in the law? Jesus said unto him, Thou shalt love the Lord thy God with all thy heart, and with all thy soul, and with all thy mind. This is the first and great commandment. And the second is like unto it, Thou shalt love thy neighbor as thyself. On these two commandments hang all the law and the prophets."

—*Jesus Christ, Matthew 22:35–40 KJV*

"I, _____ , do solemnly swear (or affirm) that I will support and defend the Constitution of the United States against all enemies, foreign and domestic; that I will bear true faith and allegiance to the same; and that I will obey the orders of the President of the United States and the orders of the officers appointed over me, according to regulations and the Uniform Code of Military Justice. So help me God."

—Oath sworn upon enlistment in the US Armed Forces

What is an example of a foreign enemy?

- What is an example of a domestic enemy?
- Which is more dangerous and why?

Who is an example of someone with a good attitude?

- What difference does a good attitude make?

"It's not your aptitude, but your attitude which determines your altitude."

—Author unknown

"A positive attitude may not solve all your problems, but it will annoy enough people to make it worth the effort."

—Herm Albright

"Attitudes are contagious. Are yours worth catching?"

—Dennis and Wendy Mannering

What is (or was) your
favorite subject in school?

• Which is (or was) your least favorite?

"It is a thousand times better to have common
sense without education than to have education
without common sense."

—*Robert G. Ingersoll, American orator*

What is your favorite color?

- What is the best example of that color you have seen?

"Actually, all education is self-education. A teacher is only a guide, to point out the way, and no school, no matter how excellent, can give you education. What you receive is like the outlines in a child's coloring book. You must fill in the colors yourself."

—*Louis L'Amour, American western novelist*

Would you die for another member of your family?

- Would you die for one of your friends?
- Would you die for a stranger?
- Would you die for an enemy?

"For scarcely for a righteous man will one die: yet peradventure for a good man some would even dare to die. But God commendeth his love toward us, in that, while we were yet sinners, Christ died for us."

—*Apostle Paul, Romans 5:7–8 KJV*

How does your family
show patriotism?

"Patriotism is as much a virtue as justice, and is
as necessary for the support of societies as natural
affection is for the support of families."

—*Benjamin Rush, US founding father*

What is the difference between a conservative, a liberal, and a libertarian?

"End results that work that don't involve government threaten liberals."

—*Rush Limbaugh, political commentator*

"One of the overriding points of Liberal Fascism is that all of the totalitarian "isms" of the left commit the fallacy of the category error. They all want the state to be something it cannot be. They passionately believe the government can love you, that the state can be your God or your church or your tribe or your parent or your village or all of these things at once. Conservatives occasionally make this mistake, libertarians never do, liberals almost always do."

—*Jonah Goldberg, columnist and author*

How does a conservative differ from a libertarian?

"If you analyze it I believe the very heart and soul of conservatism is libertarianism. I think conservatism is really a misnomer just as liberalism is a misnomer for the liberals—if we were back in the days of the Revolution, so-called conservatives today would be the Liberals and the liberals would be the Tories. The basis of conservatism is a desire for less government interference or less centralized authority or more individual freedom and this is a pretty general description also of what libertarianism is."

—*Ronald Reagan, fortieth US president*

Has someone in your family ever
served in a war?

- Tell of an experience he or she had.

"In war, there are no unwounded soldiers."

—*José Narosky, Argentine writer*

"This nation will remain the land of the free only
so long as it is the home of the brave."

—*Elmer Davis, American reporter*

How do you feel about gambling?

"Gambling is a method of getting nothing out of something."

—*Author unknown*

"If you ain't just a little scared when you enter a casino, you are either very rich or you haven't studied the games enough."

—*VP Pappy, author*

Have your religious beliefs
ever been shaken?

- How did you resolve the conflict?

"Question with boldness even the existence of
God; because, if there be one, he must more
approve of the homage of reason than that of
blindfolded fear."

—*Thomas Jefferson, founding father
and third US president*

TOPICS BY QUESTION NUMBER

TOPICS BY QUESTION NUMBER

TOPICS BY QUESTION NUMBER

TOPICS BY QUESTION NUMBER

TOPICS BY QUESTION NUMBER

About the
AUTHORS

JOHN & TINA BUSHMAN find their greatest joy in spending time together as a family. They are the proud parents of five wonderful children. The most rewarding moments in their family life are watching their children learn, discover and grow, whether it's in a formal setting, around the table, in the car, or on an outing. John and Tina grew up in Arizona and both attended Arizona State University, where they met and started their happily ever after.

ABOUT THE AUTHORS

John has a bachelor's degree in psychology and a master's degree in instructional technology, and has been an educator and speaker with youth and young adults for over fifteen years. John has also written the book *Impractical Grace*.

Tina studied physics and secondary education but left that season for a better one. She loves her stay-at-home status and enjoys creating and capturing fun times with her children.

The Bushmans now live in beautiful Washington State, where field trips are just around the corner.